I0142736

How the F*ck Did I Get Here?

Words to My Younger Self

Deidre Hudson

Copyright © 2023 Deidre Hudson

How the F*ck Did I Get Here? Words to My Younger Self is a registered trademark of Deidre Hudson

All rights reserved.

Published by grey sneaker

ISBN 13: 979-8-9869541-1-0

DEDICATION

Thanks to Bernie Glintz, LCSW, BCD, FAPA for the overstuffed green chair and his 6th-Spidey-Shrink Sense.

Thanks to Angela Mascenik and the badass OVIPs.

And last but not least, 3 awesome women in my life: Tameka Patterson, Serena Parham and Ms. Sheridan Gary.

What you think you become.

What you feel you attract.

What you imagine, you create.

~ Buddha

Table of Contents

Introduction

Are you tired of living on auto-pilot? Do you wake up every morning dreading the day ahead? Do you feel like there is something better out there for you but you just can't seem to reach it?

In "How the F*ck Did I Get Here?" author Deidre Hudson uses this provocative question to alter the course of her life. She takes you on her courageous journey to enlightenment and self-empowerment, where she discovered 3 key changes she needed to make to start living a life on purpose and full of intention.

This short read will inspire you to figure out what's holding you back so you can regain your power and create the life of your dreams.

Prologue

I started documenting this story as a cathartic exercise. It was a way of capturing all of the bad shit that I was feeling in the hopes that through the process of pressing words to paper, some patterns would be revealed, or new insights would be discovered to propel me out of the darkness I felt.

I like the use of ink blots imagery to help illustrate my story. Ink blots are sometimes used in psychological diagnoses to identify and analyze inner thoughts, feelings, and personality traits. In presenting something ambiguous the viewer is allowed to see whatever they want in it, through the lens of their own inner filters. Only by seeing how one views the world can they then start to change themselves and affect change in the world around them.

THE BEGINNING.

Where is here?

How the fuck did I get here?" I asked as I sat on an overstuffed green chair in the office of a psychiatrist one evening in early fall. For some reason, he didn't seem surprised to see me. I had been under his care several years ago when I needed help sorting out some family issues but abruptly ended our sessions as he got too close to uncovering the true source of my predicament. In retrospect, I think he had some sort of 6th- Spidey-Shrink-sense that knew we had unfinished business. I could almost hear him saying in the Terminator's voice, "You'll be back."

"Where is here?" he asked.

"Here" was The Land of Angst and Fear. It was the place and space I started to live from, where I was so afraid of making a mistake that feeling stagnant and trapped became my norm. I was simultaneously overwhelmed yet unimpressed by the routine that had become my life.

I used to be fearless. A non-conformist. If I wanted to do something, I did it. I never questioned whether I could or not. In fact, I would sooner think, why can't I, than be thwarted from trying new things or exploring new adventures. But somewhere, somehow, things changed. I became anxious, full of sadness and self-doubt. I questioned my every move. My head was full and bursting with thoughts that I could neither control nor circumvent. I couldn't sleep at night and struggled to get out of bed in the morning. Sometimes, I wanted to just disappear.

For the most part, things looked fine from the outside. I had my health, a satisfying career, and a beautiful family. But on the inside, things were crumbling, and I didn't know why. Luckily, I started hyperventilating with some frightening degree of regularity and decided to see a pulmonologist.

He was a douchebag.

Instead of, oh, I don't know...maybe running some tests...he advised me to see a psychiatrist, claiming there was nothing physically wrong with me. Of course, he was wrong, and a more qualified doctor subsequently uncovered the myriad of allergies that were causing my breathing problems. I remember leaving his office feeling even more despondent.

Eventually, I decided to take Dr. Douchebag's advice. Despite having my physical problems addressed, I couldn't shake the feelings of despair and dread that seemed determined to take up permanent residence in my spirit. I took a deep breath, picked up the phone, and made an appointment with my former therapist.

All too familiar with my hit-and-run pattern, my therapist rightfully asked me about my level of commitment. I decided that I would stick with it. I was going to fully commit to the process and figure this stuff out once and for all. No matter how uncomfortable the conversations became or how deeply we probed, I wanted the uncomfortable mirror held up to my face. I wanted to understand why I felt like I was living on autopilot. Why I was sometimes paralyzed with fear. Why I was not living my best life.

I knew it would be difficult. I mean, really difficult. Who wants to spend an hour every week talking about all the mistakes they've made and opening up old wounds? Not me! Wasn't that why I left therapy the first time? But I also knew it would be worth the effort. If I could just figure this shit out once and for all, I could take those hard-won lessons with me into the future. I could release some space in my mind and stop being a spectator in my life.

So, I went on the journey and finally figured out what I needed to do.

LESSON #1

I needed to reclaim my power.

"The most common way people give up their power
is by thinking they don't have any."
- Alice Walker

Lesson #1

There was a point where I started to relinquish control over the decision-making in my life. I stopped deciding. I became the passenger instead of the driver. I went with the flow and started letting things happen instead of selecting the things that I wanted to occur. I accepted what I was offered instead of demanding what I needed. I call it living in the land of "Might as Well". I remember being told that phrase when I sought advice on what would become a major event in my life. It was at that moment, in that slice of time when I started accepting "might as well" as an option, that I started allowing myself to settle for less than I deserved. It predicated a downward spiral. One Might as Well thought devolved to another until it just became a way of life:

"You've been in this relationship for so long, you might as well get married."

"You've been working at this job for so long, you might as well keep it."

"You've been doing it this way for so long, you might as well continue."

See what I mean? Where does this type of thinking get you?

It lands you on the couch of a shrink in Forest Hills asking, "How the fuck did I get here?"

I'd love to get into my time machine and go back to that pivotal moment with my younger self where this stream of unconscious living began and scream, "Don't do it! Take a stand! Might as well is not an option!" But of course, that is impossible. What is possible, however, is the future and learning from the past. Now, when I even come close to veering toward "might as well" as the answer to anything, I experience such a strong reaction in my body that I practically run in the other direction.

Which led me to Lesson #2.

LESSON #2

I needed to trust my gifts.

""Control of what I say, control of what I do
And this time I'm gonna do it my way
When I was seventeen
I did what people told me
Did what my father said
And let my mother mold me
But that was long ago, I'm in control"

~ Janet Jackson

Lesson #2

I was raised to be a good girl. Obedient. Respectful. Color inside the lines. And I was. I liked having rules and following a structure. And I did it well. I received good grades in school and didn't cause trouble at home. I did as I was told. Until I went away to college. But that's another story. What I realized is that although I was raised to be obedient, I was not raised to be confident. I was not brought up to trust my judgment, develop my own viewpoint, recognize my gifts and believe in myself enough to use them.

The fearlessness that I experienced in my 20s was really an act of rebellion against the regimented thinking of my childhood. "Why can't I" became my internal mantra because for too long I had heard that I couldn't, or that I shouldn't, or some similar negative bullshit when I expressed a desire for something other than what I was told I could or should do.

Every time my wrist was (metaphorically) slapped, or when I was ridiculed for expressing an emotion or a desire, I learned that my instincts did not matter. That I was incapable of knowing what I wanted and that someone else would always have a better idea of what was right for me.

What I have learned, however, is that my instincts represent the collective voice of my gifts and will guide me to who I am supposed to be. I am creative. I am intuitive. I have a high degree of emotional intelligence. Those are my gifts. I see things differently, I feel things differently, and I experience people in a different way.

In my chosen profession of marketing, I now nurture and draw on those gifts on a regular basis. A key part of my role is leading a team, and it is a responsibility that I take very seriously because of the impact I have on the lives of other people. Bringing on new team members is especially important because of the impact on the existing team dynamics. A wrong choice can cause all hell to break loose.

While working for a multibillion-dollar global fintech company, I was part of a team that was responsible for bringing on a new member in a pivotal role. Let's call her Amanda. Due to scheduling issues, I interviewed Amanda on the phone during the hiring process but was unable to meet her in person. I told myself that it was no big deal. Everyone else seemed to be satisfied, so why upset the apple cart?

Walking into the large bustling lobby of my office building on the morning Amanda was scheduled to start, I saw a young woman at the security desk. She looked fine. There was nothing discernibly out of order. But my first thought was, "Oh no! I hope that's not her!"

It was.

Amanda lasted in that position for exactly three months.

My visceral reaction to her was so swift and strong that I knew something was off, like a faint odor in the air or a piece of clothing that looks great but just doesn't feel right. And you know what? I was right. I can't explain it, but I've learned that this is just an ability that I have and instead of denying it or trying to dismiss it, I accept it as my gift. I rely on it; I leverage it and I embrace it. Now, to my last and most important lesson.

LESSON #3

I needed to forget about O.P.T.

"You down with O.P.P.?
Yeah, you know me. "

- Naughty by Nature

Lesson #3

Yes, you must be of a certain age to recognize lyrics from the song, "O.P.P." recorded by the 90s hip- hop group Naughty by Nature. But while being down with O.P.P. may have been fun in your 20's, caring about O.P.T. (Other People's Thoughts) in your 40's is not.

Behaving in a manner that was "too big for my britches" was a common childhood admonishment. And I realized that this antiquated and limiting way of thinking had carried over into my adulthood, manifested in my fear of O.P.T. It wasn't so much that I was *afraid* of doing something big or bold, my fear was about how other people would *interpret* what I was doing and a lot of times, that fear kept me from acting.

If I wanted to expand outside of my professional comfort zone, I would experience a sharp pang of fear that "they" thought I was being too assertive or too ambitious. If I disagreed with the consensus in a meeting, I worried others would think I was being difficult or operating outside of my lane. If I wore red nail polish instead of beige or made other non-conformist choices in my attire and hairstyle, I was sure my co-workers interpreted it as a signal of reduced credibility.

And I know we all (or most of us anyway) have some desire to fit in, to be taken seriously, and to be thought of favorably by our peers. So, I am not referring to the "normal" level of interest we have in how we are perceived by others. The level of anxiety and fear that I experienced was panic attack level. It was mind-numbing, intense, and sharp, complete with heart palpitations and foreboding thoughts of impending disaster.

There is a reason stress is often called the silent killer. The physiological reaction the body has to stress is severe. When your body senses fear, it immediately goes into fight or flight mode. Adrenaline and cortisol are released into your bloodstream. Your heart rate increases, your blood pressure rises, and increased glucose is delivered into your system. Over time, depression, weight gain, skin problems, and other more serious conditions can occur. Chronic stress is your body being in a constant state of fight or flight.

I had to do something.

I realized that asking questions was a strategy that always worked well for me. Growing up, I was frequently chastised by my mother for being belligerent, so why not apply some of that here? Just as asking the question "Why can't I?" served me so well in my 20s, I started to pose the question of "So what?" to the O.P.T.s It went a little something like this:

O.P.T.: She's overstepping her bounds or being too ambitious.

Me: So what? Should I continue to dim my light to make others feel comfortable?

O.P.T.: She's going against the consensus and being difficult.

Me: So what? Isn't raising questions to get the best results a part of my job?

O.P.T.: She's not dressing like everyone else. Not sure if we can trust her.

Me: So what? Judge me by my work not the way I style my hair or the color I paint my nails.

I was on to something! By responding to the O.P.T. with irreverence instead of fear, the power structure started to change. In my mind, O.P.T. had been this dark, amorphous cloud that appeared, blossomed, and followed me around like a Peanuts character's rain cloud. Trying to ignore it didn't work. Trying to push it aside didn't work. It was only when I started to question its validity did things begin to change.

I was on fire! My childhood belligerence kicked in and I started asking even more questions, like:

"Is it true? Are they really thinking this?" How the fuck should I know.

"Are they right? Am I trying too hard?" To be successful, there is no such thing as trying too hard.

"Does it matter?" At the end of the day, does someone else's opinion of me ever really matter more than my own? Nope.

By understanding that I had the power to confront O.P.T. I could let the air out of its tires and minimize the amount of space it was occupying in my brain. I realized that I didn't need to worry about O.P.T. I needed to worry about my own thoughts. Because it is through my thoughts that I can create the identify I wanted to have and regain control over my life.

The quickest way to ruin a dish is to have too many cooks in the kitchen. Thanksgiving and Christmas were big holidays in my family, and we looked forward to my mother's roast turkey and giblet gravy all year. But as my mom aged and could no longer cook a full holiday meal, she took on a supervisory role. And supervise she did. As my sisters and I worked together in the family kitchen on each holiday eve, preparing the dinner we would all consume the next day, we were required to follow her instructions to perfection. She had honed those ingredients and proportions over decades, and we were not allowed to mess with the formula by trying to put our imprints on her creations.

I believe we are supposed to be a blessing to other people. I believe we all have a calling, and it is our responsibility to fulfill that calling to the best of our abilities. But it is impossible to fulfill our true purpose and become a blessing to others if our individual recipes are muddled. I had to stop letting O.P.T. ruin the dish that God had created in me.

The sum of what I have learned, what my younger self retaught me, and what my future self will bring on our journey, is that we have much more power than we think. Nothing is written in stone and there is no invisible magic thread pulling us through life by our belly button. If we are conscious, we have a choice. The stories that we tell ourselves, and the inner worlds we create, are all up to us. And our external worlds are a direct reflection of the thoughts and feelings we stitch together internally. It all begins with a thought. So, if you can have negative thoughts that are not creating the outcomes you want, you can create new ones. We truly do have the power to create the destiny we desire.

"And one day she discovered that she was fierce

and strong, and full of fire and that not even she

could hold herself back because her passion burned brighter than

her fears."

- **Mark Anthony, poet**

Use the next few pages to take notes to yourself.

Describe how you currently feel and how you want to feel. What's keeping you from living the life you want?

ABOUT THE AUTHOR

Deidre Hudson is on a never-ending quest for living the best life possible. She is an avid proponent of lifelong learning, individual empowerment, and the art of authenticity. As a marketer that has worked with some leading consumer and B2B brands, she is able to combine her interests in creative expression and understanding the psychology of the human mind. Deidre makes her home in New York City and can be reached via LinkedIn at linkedin.com/in/deidrehudson

www.ingramcontent.com/pod-product-compliance
Lightning Source LLC
LaVergne TN
LVHW010033070426
835508LV00005B/308